Floppy's ABC

Written by Roderick Hunt

Illustrated by Alex Brychta

OXFORD

UNIVERSIT

Aa

apple

Gran picked an **apple**.

Bb

ball

Chip kicked the **ball**.

Cc

cat

Kipper likes the **cat**.

Dd

door

Biff came to the **door**.

Ee

egg

Chip had some **eggs**.

Ff

fish

Wilf went to catch a **fish**.

Gg

goldfish

Dad gave the children a **goldfish**.

Hh

hat

Kipper put on this big **hat**.

Ii

ice cream

Kipper likes **ice cream**.

Jj

jam

Dad spooned in strawberry **jam**.

Kk

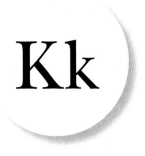

king

Chip was a **king** in the play.

Ll

leaf

Floppy ran after a **leaf**.

Mm

mirror

Kipper looked in the **mirror**.

Nn

net

Wilf had a bucket and a **net**.

Oo

octopus

The **octopus** sat on the chest.

Pp

paint

Oh no! Floppy walked in the **paint**.

Qq

queen

Gran met a **queen**.

Rr

rabbit

Kipper stroked the white **rabbit**.

Ss

sandcastle

The children made a **sandcastle**.

Tt

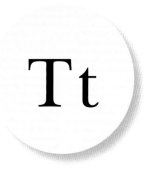

tent

Wilf showed Chip his new **tent**.

Uu

umbrella

Biff held the big **umbrella**.

Vv

vase

The children gave Gran a **vase**.

Ww

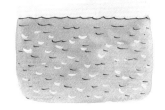

water

Dad had a bucket of **water**.

Xx

box

Lots of words end in **x**!

Kipper hid in a **box**.

Yy

Nadim gave a big **yawn**.

Zz

Chip and Wilf saw some **zebras**.

Talk about the alphabet

What letter does your name begin with?

What letters do your friends' names begin with?

What are the letters in this name: **Floppy**?

Can you find something beginning with the letter '**d**'?

29

Here is the alphabet

Point to a letter and say its name (e.g. **bee**).
Then say its sound (e.g. **buh**).

ants a b c d e f

g h i j k l

m n o p q r

s t u v w x

y z

30